THE HORRORS OF A SUCCESSFUL MARRIAGE

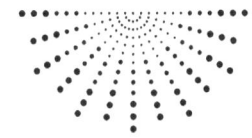

A. A. GAROFALO

Copyright © 2023 by A. A. Garofalo

All rights reserved.

Front and back cover artwork by the author.

Oil on canvas

Published by Red Penguin Books

No part of this book may be reproduced in any form or by any electronic or mechanical means, including information storage and retrieval systems, without written permission from the author, except for the use of brief quotations in a book review.

I dedicate my book

to the Holy Family,

My wife Rose

and

Annie, Rose's childhood friend who brought us together.

CONTENTS

Introduction vii

Chapter 1   1
Chapter 2   5
Chapter 3   15
Chapter 4   19
Chapter 5   25
Chapter 6   29
Chapter 7   33
Chapter 8   39
Chapter 9   45
Chapter 10   51
Chapter 11   59
Chapter 12   67
Chapter 13   79
Chapter 14   85

Good Morning!
This is God!

I will be handling
All of your problems today.
I will not need your help.
So, relax…
And have a great day!

(author unknown)

INTRODUCTION

CHAPTER ONE

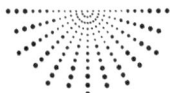

Monday evening, 6/10/2019, about 8:00 pm —first attempt at writing this book.

I am not sure where or how to start this book, so I decided to begin briefly with my four-year service in the U.S. Navy.

When I first started to talk about enlisting, my mom was very upset. She had already lost a son, Vito, who was killed in action at Iwo Jima less than one year after his enlistment in the U.S. Marine Corp. Moms of that war era were very frightened and worried, but they were of strong faith and relied on heavy-duty prayer. Our dads, although quite weary, were very supportive, compassionate and loving.

I explained to my mother my reasoning and decision that now was the best time to enlist because it was peacetime. I was 21 years of age, would eventually be drafted, and would someday like to get married, but not while I was in service. So mom prayed about it and after a while gave me her approval. On 1/1/56, I was accepted into the U.S. Navy, and our group of enlistees was sent to Bainbridge MD Naval Boot Camp for three months of basic training.

After boot camp, we were given two weeks' leave. Mom was happy; she was feeling better about it. My orders were to board a destroyer escort (DE418 USS Tabberer) in Newport, RI. We sailed the next morning and from then on we spent most of my four years at sea.

When I was discharged on 1/1/60, I had already planned on a landscape business. I had taken several correspondent courses from I.C.S. Soil Horticulture and Landscape Design which I continued to study at Farmingdale Evening College after I got started in the business.

I bought a 1951 Ford dump truck before I left the Service from Mole Ford in Amityville. The dealer was Mr. Frazer who remembered me from years gone by. When I explained my situation to him, he personally picked out the truck and held it for me for four months. He would check it occasionally. He would run the engine so as to keep her ready to go come January 1960. He did all that for me because of my service and because of the time—an era when people were very tuned in to kids and neighbors. PS: I paid $650 with no down payment required.

For the next three months, I worked for a boat builder (Sumner Craft) in Amityville. Mr. Sumner wanted me to stay with his firm. He planned to move the company to LA and offered me a position to relocate. The offer was very tempting; but my dad, after retiring that February from Republic Air Craft Co., was excited about the plans for the new business. He was very happy to share the agricultural knowledge that he learned as a child growing up in Italy, before immigrating to America at the age of 21.

PS: The first customer in my new business was Mr. Sumner. He gave me a good start with a bunch of work around his home and the factory. (Thanks, Mr. Sumner.)

CHAPTER TWO

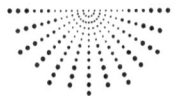

Now I need to introduce my faithful, loving wife, Rose.

Rose is loving, caring, giving, faithful, sharing, and totally committed to her trust in God and the love for her home and family. She would always extend herself in order to help anyone in any way possible, including sharing her strong commitment to the Holy Spirit and Blessed Mother—and the prayers she offers to anyone in need. When a situation would come up which was quite troublesome, she would say, "Let's pray about it," whether it be for me or any of our children or for anyone who would approach Rose. She had that special sense to know someone was in need of prayer and was always very compassionate and very sincere to any person in need.

. . .

How I met Rose:

My dad loved to grow all kinds of vegetables and was very successful at it. He would give away all that was not needed for our family. Papa would get up extra early before going to work with Mr. Damico, our neighbor who would drive him to work. My father gave up driving around 1948 when he felt there were too many cars on the road.

Papa was known as the man with the best veggies in town and also as a very sharing, caring person.

One of the customers on his little route, Mrs. Annie, got to know Papa very well; and occasionally, they would talk with each other. Papa mentioned that I would be getting home soon from my four years in the U.S. Navy and that we were starting a landscape business.

Some time lapsed and in the early Spring of 1961, Papa and I were asked to do some landscaping work for Mrs. Annie. While we were there working, she offered us coffee with her pure hospitality and then started asking me the classic, typical questions.

- Married? *No.*

- Keeping Company? *No.*

- Going to live in Copiague? *Not sure.*

- Would you like to meet a nice girl? *No, not now.*

• Why not? I *just started my business, don't have a car, and need to buy clothes. Above all, I need to concentrate on building my business. I need lots of equipment, tools and, above all, I have to build up a clientele.*

I really didn't feel that this would be the time to meet Rose.

A few weeks later I had to go back to the job to finish a small detail. At that time, Mrs. Annie invited me for Sunday dinner and quite frankly said she would like me to meet Rose and her parents, and it would be the only way that I would be able to meet her.

I was somewhat apprehensive and I needed a little time to think. I had some dress clothes, above all a white shirt and tie, blazer, new slacks, new shoes.

Back in the day, men were expected to dress that way. And the women always dressed elegantly. It would echo an air of respect and, of course, all our parents were very watchful for little signs of caring. They felt that a lot of little things equaled one good or one bad thing. Well, I didn't have a car and it was about two miles from home to Mrs. Annie's house. I called and accepted the invitation. 3 pm. I was ready to go, so I drove my "Betsy" dump truck to a few blocks from Mrs. Annie's house and walked the rest of the way.

I met Rose's parents. Dinner went well. I was asked the regular questions that parents would ask of a stranger calling on their daughter. After coffee, Mrs. Annie tried to motion to me to ask Rose if she and I could go for a walk. I was a little apprehensive but finally said to them about going. Her Mom had a little to say but was okay with it.

When we left the house, I wanted to go south because my "Betsy" was parked down the street with bright yellow letters on a green truck (Garofalo Landscape Co.) Who could miss not seeing that? Rose wanted to see this old house that she remembered from years ago as a child when her family would come out to the island for summer vacation.

Rose was born and raised in Manhattan until about 18 years of age. Her mom and dad built a home in West Hempstead on Cherry Valley Avenue where she lived until we married 5/12/62.

Rose really didn't know much about me and only a few things which we discussed on our walk. Such as—I wanted to go to evening classes at Farmingdale Agricultural College, did not own a car, need to buy a ton of equipment, trying to build up a name and steady customers, not having any medical insurance, property damage insurance, no employees, just Papa and me. So with all that, it was kinda gloomy.

As for Rose, she worked in the Mortgage Department at Franklin National Bank which does not exist any longer. She was very devoted to her parents and was the finest daughter any parent could have. Her Aunt Mary, who Rose was very fond of, would take her to church every Sunday and many other tasks. She kept in touch with all the other aunts, uncles, cousins, etc. Rose's dad (Papa Frank) was always busy with his restaurant/bar on 8th Avenue & 26th Street where he spent many long hours.

Papa Frank did all he could to keep the business going. He had to be very careful who would walk in off the street for people involved with drugs, etc. Through all of that, he was extremely charitable to the poor people. He knew who to give money to and who to feed generously. It was funny to see him sit some poor guy down, tell him not to move, and go back to the kitchen and make a huge Dagwood Bumstead Triple Decker Sandwich for the person. It had to be very rewarding for Papa Frank to see the look on that guy's face.

There are many other things which Papa was remembered for, especially family—he brought just about all of his family here from Italy, gave them places to stay, got them jobs and a really good start, gave them pride and independence. Later on in years, as it sometimes goes with family (not appreciated by some) meaning when a few times due to Papa's ailing health and other bad luck, not all were so quick to help him.

More will follow about Papa Frank later on.

Rose and her mom did most of the Visiting—old-school duty (keeping the peace.)

After The Initial "Getting To Know You Scenario"

By the way, Rose got a charge over my mode of transportation. And when we finished the little bit of laughter, she never made me feel embarrassed, and I felt very good about what we shared when we got back to Annie's house. Everything was good. We talked at the table with everyone for a while. Then I thought it was time for me to leave. Did my respectable good nights, thanked Annie, thanked Mr. & Mrs. Lobascio (was a pleasure to meet you) and I went home.

After that day, I had many thoughts about Rose, but my concerns with trying to do all the things that needed to be done—my things—had to take first priority.

A short time after the "Rose and Gus Day," Annie called me (not at Rose's request). I came to find out later that Rose would never call any guy, including me, not for any kind of follow up. I truly felt that of Rose and I admired her for it (old-school). Again I explained to Annie of my situation: a) I did not have a steady income, b) I had no health insurance. I didn't know if I always had steady contracts. I needed more equipment and was starting to feel the crunch of creditors. Plus, I didn't even have a car. So, Annie, I love you and I know you understand.

Some time went by and I met Annie by chance in town (Copiague). We spoke some more—this time she gave me Rose's phone number. I never realized how much time went by and that I misplaced her phone number.

Not realizing that almost one year went by from our first meeting, I felt I should call Annie and explain, and also find out if Rose had been engaged or seeing anyone at that time. Annie said she would find out for me.

I was starting to get busy, more contracts, more steady clientele, new complete types landscape, commercial and residential. I was able to hire two men which were a great help for Papa.

In the beginning, things were really going good. I was offered the opportunity by a rep from MotoRake Corp. to demonstrate a new machine for lawn care, and whatever money came in from it, I was to keep. I had to give weekly reports to the field rep on:

1. Explaining the machine to the customer

2. Explaining the benefits of the process

3. When best to do the work

4. How effective was the demo

5. Machine performance at the time of demo

6. In all cases, the process sold itself

Good to know Mr. Charles Inc. (Amity Feed Supply) had recommended me for that opportunity. (Thanks Mr. C.)

PS: The MotoRake became very popular and is known today as Power Raking. Every landscaper offers the additional service now.

Again, more time went by. Annie did speak to Rose, and she said it was okay to call her. I did call Rose a few days later. We spoke for over one hour. In that time spent, I had a feeling that my footloose and fancy-free days were over. After that, again I faded, but not for too long. Then, ironically, my Papa had to go prune some fruit trees by Mrs. Annie's house. When he came home, he said, "Glad you met a very nice girl. We would love to meet her, too." Okay, Papa, soon. Now Papa got me thinking.

I called Annie and explained that I had no car, felt ridiculous in a strange neighborhood on a Sunday afternoon in bright daylight parking a large, beat-up dump truck in front of 42 South Cherry Avenue in West Hempstead. I was nervous and didn't know how her parents would perceive the situation.

So Annie offered to lend me her car. I really did not want to borrow it. My two brothers-in-law offered their car. I felt better with that, so I called Rose again. We spoke for a while. She asked me over for Sunday dinner. It was okay with her parents. It was great to know that we would finally see each other again. At one point in time, we had a mutual feeling for each other.

Everything went well that day, including the customary scrutiny toward me by her aunts and other friends of the Lobascio family, but I did understand how strict Italian families dealt with new changes in their homes. P.S. Mine was the same and all of that European culture, it's ok.

Rose told me not to worry. I already had Papa Frank's approval, and Rose was quite attentive to me. I don't want it to sound like a Horror Show—it wasn't. It was routine. However, it can be a little pressing when you are the only stranger at the dinner table amongst caring, concerned, etc. family, especially when a member of the family (Rose) is possibly making plans for her future.

(Mom) Lobascio had her thoughts—I am losing a daughter; I won't see you anymore; He is taking you away, etc. All those thoughts come from a sincere strong love for her Rosie. And, none of those things ever happened. (This will be discussed later on.)

CHAPTER THREE

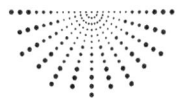

*N*ow! On to my Family

Mom and Papa Garofalo hadn't seen Rose for quite a while after Rose and my first formal meeting. They didn't say too much, but my four sisters were curious for information. At that time, all I could say to them was Rose and I spoke a lot. We had much in common—our religious beliefs, we both went to parochial school, had a great work ethic, loved family and all that other good stuff. Now, considerable time had passed where I failed to contact Rose, and Annie had been asking me at times how did we leave off with each other. Again! I explained my situation to her and asked her as politely as I could to please leave it alone. Then I came to find out that some of the girls that Rose worked with were encouraging her to telephone me. As I explained earlier, Rose would never call any guy unless there was a strong commitment to each other. (Got to love it.)

I won't get into the Millennial Era, but this small attribute did exist 60 years ago, along with many other good behavioral traits. More later about traits.

So more time went by and another attempt by Annie for me to call Rose. Well, I thought about it, thinking it was just about one year since we met. And all which had passed by so fast.

I decided to call Annie to get some Intel (how things were) with Rose. Annie was delighted to hear that I wanted to talk to Rose again not knowing of her status with any engagements, or anyone serious with her.

Annie called Rose to see if it was okay to give me her phone number. Rose said okay. Annie did her part, informed me of OK. Got her phone number.

I waited a day or two because I was nervous. When I finally called her towards the end of the week, we spoke for a while. All seemed okay so I asked if I could come over to see her. Well, no girl wants to entertain a guy with an ice pack on her jaw due to having an impacted wisdom tooth removed, but knowing Rose, later on, she was okay with it.

I told Annie all was good. She was so happy. She immediately offered her car to me, but my brother-in-law Russ offered. It was set for that Saturday night. I brought her a bouquet of flowers, said my hellos to Mom and Rose, got reacquainted. Then I felt very comfortable, not at all nervous with Rose. We made a few funny gestures about her swollen jaw and began talking about a lot of things (Mom always present). A little while later on, Rose made a pot of coffee for us. She set up the kitchen table so homelike, with cups and saucers, napkins, a tray of cookies which she baked, milk, sugar and a lot of care (God bless you, Rose).

I was always a little shy about eating in front of strangers to the point of when Rose asked me if I wanted milk and sugar, I said no. They both commented about my choice, so I said I recently started to drink it black for a better taste of the coffee. But the truth of the matter is I was too shy to ask for the milk and sugar, but I did manage to eat a couple of Rosie's homemade cookies. Later on, I did tell Rose that the story about milk and sugar was not true.

The evening went really well. I asked Rose if I could see her again; she said yes. Then shortly after that, Mom said, "Well sonny, it's 10:30. I have to go to work tomorrow, so say goodnight." And she waited until I got up, said thank you for your hospitality, Good Night.

I was not offended. I guess it was that I had a strong feeling for Rose. And again, I recognized the thoughtfulness of mom and her waiting for a response.

I did feel a little strange because we were both adults, I was 25 and Rose was 24. Moms of that era, numbers meant nothing to them—you will always be their baby. Including my Mom.

After a couple of dates with Rose, my family started asking me about Rose and her family, mostly my sisters. Mom and Dad never pressured me, except for Rose's religion (being Catholic); but Mom, Isabel, Rose, and Antionette had changed their faith; they followed Mom. When Vito was killed at war, she took it bad enough that she turned from her faith. A close friend (Anna) who loved mom dearly, asked her to come to one of her Full Gospel Assembly Church services. The people greeted Mom so warmly that Mom continued to go with Anna, and Mom started to feel better about everything.

After a while, my three sisters became inspired and began going regularly. Prior to that, they never were really committed to any faith, except Margaret. As for me, once I started my position in my Catholic school education, they didn't bother me too much.

CHAPTER FOUR

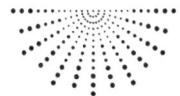

*R*ose and I continued to date. I bought a 1953 Ford 4-door—I think it was a Fairlane. Things were going well and I nervously asked Rose about getting engaged. We talked for a while. We felt that we knew enough about each other and our family's finances. I did stipulate that we needed to live around the Copiague-Lindenhurst area because of my business, that I rented property and building for my equipment. All was okay with Rose.

With all that behind us, we went looking for an engagement ring. Rose didn't want the Hope Diamond, but a perfect blue-white diamond about 60 points, white gold solitaire setting. My sister Margaret told us about Cousin Carlo Cafaro who was a jeweler in Garden City. We got in touch with him and Rose picked out the ring. Cousin Carlo treated us really well.

I asked my cousin to please let me know when the ring would be ready because I wanted to surprise Rose in a special way. Shortly, thereafter, my cousin Carlo called to tell me the ring was ready. I picked it up later the same day.

I knew that Rose went to 8 am Mass at St. Catherine of Sienna Church in Franklin Square every morning before going to work. So the very next morning, I got up extra early, got dressed and got to church in time. Mass had just started. I saw where Rose was sitting. I paused for a moment, a little nervous. Then I went right to her, kneeling next to her, gave a greeting. She was very surprised, if not shocked, to see me. I had to wait for a certain time during Mass (the offertory). Then I gave her the ring. We both were so happy at that moment. We could not say too much in church. We just felt so close together.

When Mass was over, I walked Rose to work. All we did was talk about the way all things happened. 'Til this day, 57 years later, we share our/my proposal in conversation with anyone (came in handy at Pre-Cana in-home class Rose and I taught.) More about PreCana later.

The engagement brought us a feeling of closeness and we wanted to be always together. There was much to be done. We still didn't set a date and a lot of other things were happening.

Then we announced our engagement to everyone. We did not have a date set yet. Of course, everyone was excited to know when.

Now Rose and I were trying to get a date set for our parents to meet at my house in Copiague. Our families were happy for us, gave us many blessings and best wishes.

We finally all agreed on Sunday—I don't remember the exact date, but it was in the early part of December.

Dinner went well. Both parents expressed their feelings towards us and agreed that we were wise enough to realize the commitment and effort which lay ahead.

My three sisters Isabel, Rose, and Antoinette were a bit stand-offish during dinner and after that, I could sense Margaret's concerns for Rose and me. I knew that she would address the three of them. As time went on, we saw each other more frequently and my parents always asked for Rose. It wasn't easy for her to come out to visit because her dad always entertained on weekends and he relied on Rose to host the visits. I was free to come and go home. My parents never interfered with me. However, they always said we would love to see Rose at any time.

I was invited every weekend by Papa Frank, and I would go just to be with Rose. When you sat down with Papa Frank at the dinner table, it was usually an all-day affair. There were times we did manage to get away for a while and be able to enjoy each other and talk about our plans.

My sisters, on occasion, would needle me about my time spent with Rose and I should bring her around more often. I told them, "When you can make my future wife feel comfortable and wanted by you three, I would gladly share her with you." Not too much was said after that.

Rose and I decided it was time to choose a wedding date. In January of 1962, we both agreed on May 12, 1962. Rose wanted to honor the Blessed Mother, and May is her month.) We announced it to everyone. There was a lot of excitement for Rose, a lot of God Bless You's, Best Wishes, *"Buona Fortuna,"* etc. Rose never had an engagement party, so Mamma Lena gave Rose a bridal shower which turned out very well.

We started looking for apartments out around Copiague. I was working for a builder as a carpenter in my offseason. Mr. Staleto gave me tons of landscape in season. One of my jobs one day was to replace a broken pane of glass, a brand new dormer apartment that had never been rented. I inquired about it from the owners and explained it to Rose. She was anxious to see it. We got an appointment with the owners. Rose loved it. The owners told us as newlyweds, they would give it to us for $125 a month which included electric and heat. One great stroke of luck.

We continued to make plans for the church, St. Thomas the Apostle in West Hempstead, the reception hall, Rose for her gown, bridesmaids and their gowns, my best man, flowers, limos, music, my Mom, Pop and Sisters, my tux, my two workers, and our honeymoon. One of Rose's friends—Dorothy and her husband—recommended Cove Haven on Echo Lane in PA. The package included your own cabin, breakfast served at your time request, all meals, all activities. We were very pleased with it and the price was good for us.

Through Rose's Papa, who was familiar with lots of people in his type of business, Papa Frank asked us to go with him to this catering place named Tufaro's in Corona, Queens. We liked it. Of course, it was nothing like the places that exist today. Mr. Tufaro showed Rose and me around. He reviewed the menu which had three choices for the entree (Prime Rib, Chicken any style, Pasta) all complete with a choice of vegetables, wine, beer, soda and a Viennese hour. 57 years ago the price was $7.95 per plate. $125 for live music. Thanks to Papa Frank, we took it.

My family (sisters, mom, and dad) didn't have to worry about transportation as Margret and Ann both had husbands to bring them to the church and reception. As time was getting closer, we started our guest lists which were 140 guests between both families. No problem.

Narrowing it down, the list remained at 140.

I was back in full swing with my business. Rose was getting calls from some people stating: I hope I can make it; please don't seat me at the same table with so and so; If you-know-who shows up, I am not coming. Very, very stupid, but Papa Frank looked into it for us.

I don't say I wouldn't have the same problem, but we didn't have very many relatives here in New York. They were all in Chicago and those who could attend did. Unfortunately, those things still happen today, mostly at weddings and wakes.

After all that baloney, we continued to plan. Things were going well except for Isabelle and Rose giving Mom a hard time over the two aunts coming from Chicago. They did not want them to stay at our house. Poor Mom was so upset over this, she didn't know what to do. But I knew what had to be done. I warned Isabelle and Rose that I would tell Papa, who knew nothing about it; and they knew Papa would end it *"pronto."* Well, they left Mamma alone, and anyway, they took my bedroom and I took the couch. All remained quiet, thank God. Everything settled down. No more major problems. We found time for Rose to visit Mom and Pop. They were happy; they both really loved Rose.

CHAPTER FIVE

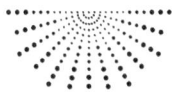

*A*round April 18th, Papa and I were doing some work not far from home. Papa wasn't feeling too well, so I took him home and by then he was pretty much in pain. He did have an ongoing problem with stomach ulcers. I left him with Mom and 2 sisters, and I went back to the job site to pick up a tractor and other equipment and to release our helpers. By the time I got home, my sister had already called the ambulance to take him to Brunswick General Hospital in Amityville because of his severe pain.

I was living at home at that time on Beachview Street in Copiague, Long Island, a house that my parents were able to buy after many years. But it came with a stipulation -- the gentleman (widower) who was the seller had to live with us until his death. We had to put an extension on the house for all of us to be able to live there. All was good with that scenario.

Now, when I got home and found that they had rushed Papa to the hospital, I went there immediately. The staff had set Papa up for emergency surgery, but because of his medical benefits, we needed a $300 copay for admittance. Luckily, I had a blank check with me.

They rushed Papa into surgery and found that he had a perforated ulcer. After nearly three hours in surgery, the lead surgeon came to us and explained that they were able to correct the perforation in his stomach, but he was listed as critical. He was in and out of a coma, but then sank deeper into the coma and developed peritonitis which he could not overcome, and passed away April 24, 1962—18 days prior to our wedding.

It was a devastating time not just for Rose and me being so close to our wedding; but many other things. He was only 67 years of age, had finally retired after many years of working, finally owned his own home, and Papa and I starting off together. How happy he was and looking forward to the wedding and many other things which we all knew about. And Mom, grief-stricken with thoughts of losing the love of her life, best friend, her go-to guy and each other's "One and Only Love".

Now Rose and I had some very difficult problems to deal with. Of course, invitations were sent. The reception hall was reserved, Musicians, bridesmaids' gowns, limo, church and priest, men's tuxes, best man, flowers for church and reception, honeymoon package.

There was some pretty heavy opposition from family, meaning my sisters, not Margaret. Mama was just listening and wondering. I never wanted to put the question to Mama. How she alone felt about us going ahead or not.

Rose and I decided to talk to Father Murphy who was going to perform the blessed Sacrament for us. We asked for his input.

Father Murphy came up with a suggestion which we both thought was fine. It was this: If anyone here feels heavy-hearted or is being disrespectful towards John and family and could not participate in the festivities, the music, and the dancing will not start until 10 pm. If you feel the need to leave at that time, your choice is perfectly understandable by the family of Papa John.

Knowing from Gus and Rose how excited Papa was patiently looking forward to the day, he would not want it any other way. Thank you, Father Murphy (Gus and Rose).

CHAPTER SIX

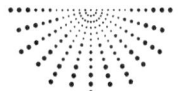

The wedding went on as planned. My Mama and sisters left at 10 pm along with a few other people. There was never any bad remarks made. As a matter of fact, Rose and I were complimented on getting good advice and using it.

I am perfectly content with our decision.

Rose and I stayed to the end. We brought a change of clothes. Our car was all packed and ready to go. Just before leaving, Rose and I had to take care of the balance of the reception. As we both agreed to pay for it due to the financial circumstances of both our parents. We thanked everyone for such a wonderful reception, and they all sent us off with good luck and God's blessings.

We arrived at Cove Haven around 4 am; our cottage was ready for us. We were quite exhausted, left a note with the desk that we would probably get a late breakfast which we did. The days' activities were great, but Rose could sense that I was still heavyhearted over my father and she was very patient with me. I did my best to get over it not to let it hurt us or take away from our most precious time together. We were enjoying our honeymoon, especially finding out so much more about each other. We wished that we could stay much longer, but (duty calls) we left Cove Haven on the morning of May 19th and drove directly to our new apartment.

During the time after the bridal shower, we were able to bring the gifts and pretty much set up with everything for a great start. So when we arrived in town (Copiague), we picked up a few items of food. We had phone service, we had taken care of it while setting up our apartment. We both made several calls to tell everyone we were home.

I don't remember the exact day, but Rose didn't go back to work until the following Monday. I went back sooner due to customer obligations. After we visited everyone, family and friends, we got quite a few invitations for dinner and just to be in the company. We did our best not to slight anyone and we thank God it all worked out well.

My sister Margaret and her husband, Jim, lived in Amityville about a half-mile away. Antoinette and her husband, Russ, lived 8 blocks away from us. They were very hospitable to Rose. I was very happy to have that wonderful satisfaction. It was a great feeling for me. Rose and Margaret hit it off very well. Antoinette was never as close as Marge, but it was okay because I knew that Rose could handle herself.

CHAPTER SEVEN

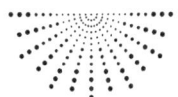

Mama, Rose, and Isabelle decided to sell the house on Beachview Street and move out to Islip Terrace where their church-owned property with four bungalows. They didn't want to make any effort to keep up the mortgage or any other responsibilities. Besides, they were very happy living on the church grounds. The Pastor treated them very well and Sister Virginia Pastor loved Mama very much. So all of us agreed on their move and that they found a great job living in that small church community.

Over time, we met most of the brothers and sisters in faith. They were mostly humble, very thoughtful of each other, loved their pastor and Mama was held very high with them. Even the children were very respectful to the elders. I took it as a good thing.

Now months have gone by, things were going well. Rose got a promotion at her job and an increase in her salary—much appreciated. My landscaping business was doing well. When I bought my tractor, I was able to sign up snow removal contracts, mostly commercial, which was also a great financial asset for us.

Mama, Rose, and Isabelle were enjoying their new religious community but there was always some resentment towards Rose and I truly believed it was due to insecurity. Mama had different feelings and they were 'If we didn't convert to their faith, we would not be saved.' Aside from everything else, the best things and the happiest thing that could happen to us was that Rose became pregnant. She was so excited to tell everyone and all were happy for us. The baby was due in September, so we started preparing our apartment. The girls at work gave Rose a surprise baby shower and Mom Lena gave one at home. No one knew in those days whether a boy or girl, so gifts were done a little differently. We did get most of the important things whether for a boy or girl. We were pretty much set for the baby's arrival. Our baby was born on 9/12/63.

Rose's prayers and her hopes were answered, feeling that this was the start for her wanting 4 or 5 children.

When John Francis Garofalo came home, with respect to his two grandfathers names—John, my Papa, and Francis, Rose's Papa. If it were a girl, she would be called Lena, for Rose's mom.

Our church was Our Lady of the Assumption in Copiague and baby John was baptized there. We had a little party for John with family and a few friends. Rose did not go back to work. She and I agreed that it should be natural for the mother to bring up the children. Anyway, it would be difficult for us to have someone else at the most crucial time of development. The people we would not hesitate to ask would be grandparents if they were physically able.

John had his regular pediatric visits. He was doing really well. Then, just before his first birthday, Rose noticed he was a little irritable, fussy eating, not sleeping well. Rose took him to the doctor. He examined him, then sent Rose downstairs for a blood test. That's when Rose suspected something more serious. With the results of the test, the doctor recommended a pediatric hematologist, Dr. Weisfuse at Booth Memorial Hospital in Flushing, New York. We were able to get a pretty quick appointment with the doctor. He reviewed the test report, and as humanly gentle as a man could be, he explained that baby John has acute leukemia [October 1964]. We were both mortified.

We felt weak in the knees and other things. The doctor suggested we should be alone for a while, and he went to check on the baby. When we finally went into the ward where he was being treated by several nurses, they were really swelling with the attention given to John.

He had to stay overnight due to having to monitor the medication. Of course, Rose was not about to go home, so they let us stay in a quiet area for the night. The entire staff was very compassionate to us. The next morning when they said it was okay to see John, we found him very comfortable but really wanting Mommy. The nurse explained that we should go home because, with our presence, his treatment would be difficult. However, she did say it would be better to come back around 3 pm.

Baby John was released later that day. Dr. Weisfuse explained that the medication would help his flu-like symptoms, but extensive blood monitoring would be needed. A few things the doctor told us to expect: irritableness, puffiness in the face and hands, more black and blue areas, very dark stool. We had baby John back and forth many times. The final medication was very powerful and he could not have more than three doses. One procedure was a spinal tap which is very painful, but very necessary. We were there for it, but before they did it, they made us leave the area so as not to hear the baby.

Baby John spent his first birthday in the hospital. The nurses gave John a little birthday party which was very thoughtful of them, and Rose and I did appreciate all that the nurses did for baby John.

We took John home again and kept in touch with Dr. Weisfuse. The visits became more frequent. We could see Johnny growing weaker. The blood transfusions were becoming very difficult due to his veins becoming harder to find. Finally, there was no more they could do for baby John.

Then, on January 30, 1965, baby John Francis passed away. He was 17 months of age. We were pretty much at peace with this due mostly for all the prayers for John, Rose and me. We were absolutely positively sure that Johnny was with Jesus and he became our own little angel. After all the funeral services, and which I am proud to say, Johnny is resting in a military site due to my service in the US Navy, which is reserved for Rose and me also.

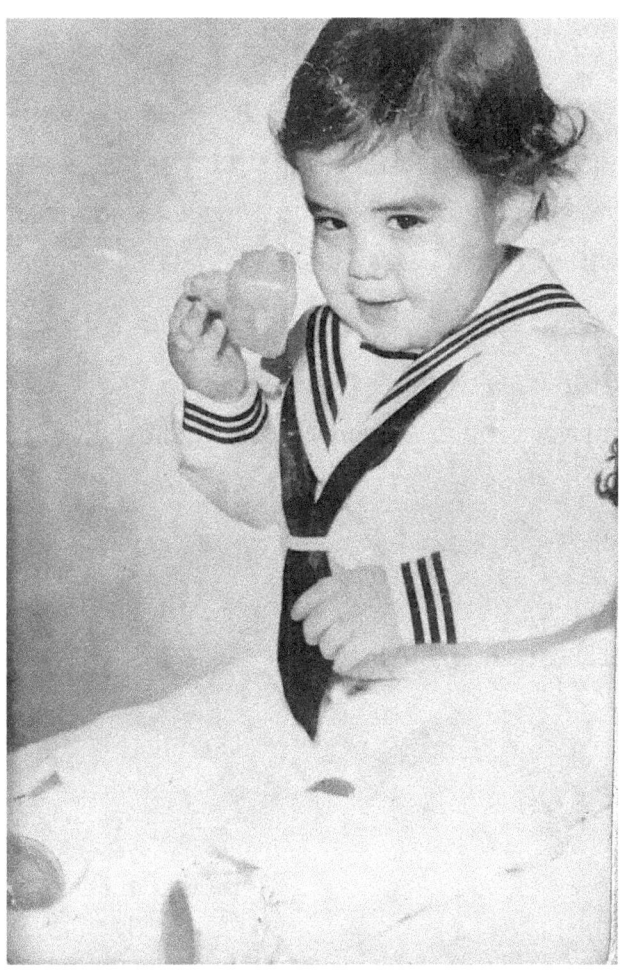

Rose didn't go back to work right away. Her pain was enormous, especially for a girl who loved children and wanted five of her own. But she kept very strong in her faith and never gave up on Jesus and the Blessed Mother. Rose and I spoke a lot many nights together. She once told me that her pain was so bad, she did not know what to do. She was very emotional and finally cried out in a loud voice to Jesus asking him for some form of peace. After a short while, she felt a very warm calmness over herself, and from then on, she dealt with her grief very differently and very much at peace.

I did whatever I could do for our situation. As I stated previously, the woman, mother of the house, has many situations to deal with. In most cases, the dad is the breadwinner, so his own grief is very different than the mom's.

Papa Frank wasn't feeling too well. He couldn't keep up his restaurant very much longer. He had to close it. Plus, he lost his liquor license thanks to his brother (not to go into detail about that.)

PS: We found out that Rose was pregnant with our baby girl Angela (Happy Happy Joy Joy)

CHAPTER EIGHT

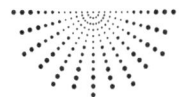

Back to Papa Frank

Rose and I thought it would be good for Pop to come out to our area. I found a small place for him to set up a sandwich and side-dish shop. I was able to get the building and property for a very reasonable rent. The landlord gave us the go-ahead to remodel any way we wanted to. It was very small. It did have a bathroom. We brought in kitchen, sink, hot water heater, deep freeze, refrigerator, gas stove, necessary lighting. I had to make a metal hood over the cooking area with an exhaust fan (all are Village of Lindenhurst requirements to get the Certificate of Occupancy.) I graded and leveled the surrounding property, finished the area off with crushed bluestone, and put a couple of picnic tables with umbrellas. The store was too small for a sit-down area.

At the time, Rose and I were looking for a house in our area. I was called by a builder, Mr. G., for two new houses that were ready for landscape in our area. One of the houses was sold. I mentioned the other to Rose although we were looking for a low ranch. Mr. G gave me the key for us to look at it. It was very appealing to both of us and we just set it aside. We hadn't completed Pop's Shop yet, and one day I was doing some final fixings, I need some pipe fittings. So Pop took a ride with me to the hardware store. Mr. G's son, Mr. D, ran the store and Pop G ran the construction business. Papa Frank came into the store with me. He was just looking around when he called me over for me to ask Mr. G if he remembered when a certain party would call him (Frankie Paul). As soon as I said the name, his response was instantaneous to me "Who told you that?" I replied Cheech Lobascio, he is my father-in-law. He is here with me now. When they came together for the first time in approximately 35 years, it was a refreshing sight. Come to find out later on that Papa Frank helped Mr. G with some problems concerning money. They were people who would lend money at a very HIGH payback rate. They called on Mr. G once and the second time, they meant business. They had Mr. G and were ready to do some physical harm, but Papa Frank heard of it and cleared Mr. G's debt. Papa Frank told Mr. G not to worry, don't do it again, and when you can afford it, you can pay back the money.

Now Papa Frank knew that Rose and I looked at Mr. G's new house. We both liked it, but it was out of our reach at

$21,500 in 1963. Papa Frank told us to invite Mr. & Mrs. G for dinner to our apartment, and also Papa Frank would get the steaks from the butcher he knew from his area in Manhattan. All went well with dinner. While Papa Frank and Mr. G were reminiscing, I asked Mr. G if Rose and I could see the house again (he gave us the key.)

Rose and I agreed that $21,500 was too high for us, but maybe the powers that be were talking. Well sure enough, when we got back to our apartment, the first thing Mr. G asked was how did we like it. We both said we do like it. The next words spoken came from Mr. G—The one on the left is sold $22,000. Before I could say another word, Mr. G said I will give it to you for $18,500. We were speechless. Mr. G said, "Take your time. I won't sell it unless you don't want it." We thought about it for a few days and decided to go ahead with it.

Rose checked with the mortgage department at her job. All were happy for us, and the mortgage rep offered to handle our mortgage. All went well. We moved in on July 4, 1963.

Rose continued to work until Angela Marie came along on October 27, 1965. We thank God she was born very health as a Jibber Jabber redhead. She was beautiful! And still is. Angela's arrival was the best thing for Rose. There was much to look forward to, an infant to love, prayers answered, brighter days.

Papa Frank did get to enjoy baby Angela for about six months. He was admitted to the hospital in April of 1966 and was diagnosed with non-alcoholic sclerosis of the liver and passed on June 26, 1966.

Now that makes three of the most precious people to us that are gone.

Not long after Papa Frank's passing, Mom Lena had to sell the house in West Hempstead. She could not live alone, and Rose would not hear of it. The house sold within a year and we set Mom up downstairs, where she lived until her death in 1983.

While Papa Frank was in the hospital, my sisters Margaret and Ann were very good to Rose for babysitting and whatever else they could help with. I felt very good for Rose knowing she trusted the two and was not at all worried in any way. They also offered to help Rose and on many occasions, Rose would bring Angela to their homes in Westbury, Long Island which was on the way to the hospital. It all worked out very well.

Margaret and Rose were getting along really well. Antoinette still had certain resentments or jealousy issues. Three of Rose's aunts and cousins were great family—very sincere, hospitable and caring. I did not have relations here in New York. They were all in Chicago. Except for the two adult aunts who came to our wedding, Rose never met any of the others until we started to call each other and eventually started traveling. Most of us were around the same age, so it made things nice.

More great happy news. Rose was pregnant with Robert Frank who was born on October 9, 1966. We again thank God for another healthy baby. Rose and I could not have been happier.

We never asked why. We never felt anything other than the will of God was happening to us. When baby John was so sick, the medical benefits policy we had (thanks for the bad advice from the insurance agent) was not enough to cover hospital, hematologist, lab work, etc. Plus, we had just taken on a mortgage with all the other expenses. I had to sell my business completely to help pay the expenses. I took a job with Grumman Aircraft and after 6 months, I was vested. Now my family had medical benefits. I had to take on part-time work to supplement my regular pay. I put my ad in a local paper (South Bay Shopper). I got lots of work—carpentry, masonry, house painting, wallpapering, landscaping, etc. I was very lucky that God gave me the gift of working with my hands. I didn't mind all the work that I was getting, but only many hours away from my NEW family. The greatest piece of mind which kept me going was knowing how dedicated Rose was with our home and children. She never complained about the many hours that I was away and not being there to help her, and she was sympathetic to me.

CHAPTER NINE

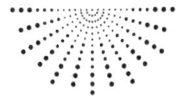

It seemed like after losing my business, everything was going downhill.

Through an employment ad I read in *Newsday*, I saw Transcarribean Airlines was hiring. The pay was much greater than Grumman and they offered medical benefits. I talked it over with Rose, and we agreed that I should go for an interview.

I got an appointment for the interview, went through it, and two weeks later received notice I was accepted and got a starting date.

After my training, they assigned me a work schedule. I was able to continue my part-time handyman work. I applied for a crew schedule position and was accepted. There was a slight increase in pay from aircraft maintenance to the new job. I really loved the job. There was a reasonable amount of overtime pay. And then the announcement came that the airline was closing down and selling to American Airlines. They gave us the option to go with the American crew schedule. I would be #42 on the seniority list with many shift changes or take severance pay which was offered by the airline. I chose the severance pay.

I applied to LILCO and was accepted and later found it was the best job I ever had in all respects, and that is where I remained until I retired in 1999 after 26 years. I thank God for my prayers being answered for finding a place like LILCO to work for. Rose was grateful because it was very secure and she liked how they treated their employees. I continued to do part-time general contract work. Later, a switch from building maintenance to a department overflowing with overtime for which we were very grateful.

We were getting along nicely. Baby Angela was doing really well, and baby Robert was on his way. Rose was in her glory just being able to feel like a real mother, homemaker and being a very fine wife. Never neglecting her little family, Rose always kept up her religious beliefs starting the babies really young about our faith. I started to slack off going to church, but Rose showed me in many different ways how important it was for the kids to see Mom as well as Dad go to church every Sunday and on holy days of obligation, and to volunteer for what you were able to do, etc.

Please excuse me for some of the things that I have already written which may not seem in order or arranged chronologically. There is simply too much in 57 years of marriage to place completely in order. In some cases and some of the events which occurred, the people involved in such events are all deceased which eliminates my best references. I will refer to some old friends or relatives wherever available.

Rose and I worked very well together in the household. Things didn't always run smoothly, we both felt we were getting to know each other more and more—seeing, doing, hearing, realizing lots of things about each other. Not liking certain things, lots of silly things which can be dangerous, some issues which were very large and dangerous, and the hardest thing for me at times was to admit being wrong, being reminded, falling back on things said, done, promised not to do again, deliberate sarcasm (which can be very painful), tardiness and lack of interest.

In spouses daily events, neglecting children, neglecting parents, any resentments toward each other. When some of these things begin to happen, sometimes it gets ignored which is not good, but not always easy to approach. When that happens, things become more difficult and more painful. I try to pass on this little helpful phrase from our Blessed Mother Mary:

If there is a disagreement and you make peace, even if you are not at fault, all of heaven will applaud you. Blessed are the peacemakers, my children this cannot be stated enough.

The older we get and I believe what I am going to say is true, I have paid particular attention to the people in our age group. Some who are dear, life-long friends and strangers (there are exceptions), the response to each other is at times quite brash. Sometimes it can be due to a hearing problem or just a nasty frame of mind. And, often the things which I mentioned are not due to old age. Also, this behavior can be brought to our children.

The purpose of this entry is to reveal that Rose and I are experiencing this condition, and in part, it has been my behavior at a much earlier age. And the only resolve is when we are alone early in the morning with our coffee and the early morning darkness as we begin our daily offering to Jesus, we recap yesterday's behavior and most of the time through my talking and Rose to listen. Then I ask her to please pardon me, then she truly understands and then I feel at peace and so happy that all is good. We try to see what causes the brash behavior and we or I reflect on our difficult times which can also trigger a lousy mood change. We never ran away from anything financial, family or any other. There were so many things we would like to have had, places to go, events to attend, etc. Then, there were the small things and lots of them. For example, why did you leave the light on, probably all day in the garage, water running in the bathroom sink, or you left your shoes where I tripped over them, or why didn't you call my sister, or why did you forget what I wanted at the store. These are small occurrences that can grow into ugly problems and must be addressed with care and love and sincerity. And there are many, many more of those devil-inspired dangerous things.

As of May 12, 2019, we managed 57 years and still encounter some of the old problems and some new. But we never closed on any of the problems until we were both satisfied and agreed that we were both pleased with the outcome. I have to admit that Rose was a haunt with all things concerning our new God-given family.

We also felt terrible about so many marriages failing in so little time of the bond, and the very small reason given, which in all probability with proper counsel could have been avoided. Rose and I have had many serious problems with family which could have interfered with our marriage, but by the saving grace of God, we overcame them because of our sincere trust in each other.

There are many, many good solid marriages out there, and we kinda like to feel that these marriages have some religious commitment. After all, marriage is a blessed, holy sacrament, and if we hold on to that fact, we would be better off.

Reflecting back on some of the things I would like to have had but couldn't at the time, and did cause some problems, but again as difficult as it was for me to accept and having to accept the discouragement, and feeling down because we could not afford what I wanted, I started to feel that all the extra hours and handyman work I was doing, that there was no end in sight. Unless it was a tool that I needed or some car repair, everything else was out of reach. So again, we would go into some real serious talk, I would brood about the facts and sometimes take a while before I realized that there were much more very important things which had to come first. I thank God for Rose's patience with me, and I came to realize there were lots of things she would like to have too, but she never really complained. There were many birthdays, graduations, christenings, confirmations, anniversaries, bridal showers, weddings, baby showers, Christmas giving, etc. These were obligations that we did our best to fulfill. Then there were times we had to make social visits when we were invited for Sunday dinner to friends or family. There were times I did not want to go, but these are obligations to share whether we liked it or not. Then there was an illness at home, family, and friends. There were so many things which could change your plans. Any time that the phone would ring, it could be a relative or close friend asking to keep a certain date open for whatever, and lots of times, 2 to 4 things could take place in one month. We would both agree that we needed a break, but that was also difficult to do.

There are many more things that can have a very adverse effect on your behavior toward that beautiful union consecrated by God for you and your best lady. As I have stated earlier, I don't have things exactly timed.

CHAPTER TEN

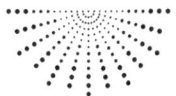

Going back to my childhood, I was really not ever sports-minded. I never knew my brother except that he and his friend Dominic loved horses and would work around the stables all day and would get to ride for free in return for their work. My Dad loved to read Italian novels and knew most of the most famous operas by heart. My best friends (Jerry, Jackie, Hugh, Sonney, and Billy) would play football with a tightly rolled-in-a-special-way newspaper and hold together with friction tape.

As a result, I didn't have much experience with sports to share with my children. Whenever I could, I would attend their events and I would cheer them on and show my pride in them. Rose was always there for them and explain that Dad needed to work to be able to keep up the necessities that were needed.

We passed through that period and, by the grace of God, my children realized that things were how they had to be. Also, as they grew older, they didn't have any resentments. Again, I was very proud of them and, not knowing what was to become of them, so we always prayed that the Holy Family would look over them.

Then, in February 1974, another Garofalo came into our world and most welcomed, Christopher. Now Rose, well we have 3 out of 4 and if God wants, there will be 4 out of 5. However, she was toxic with Chris and the doctors advised not to have any more.

Christopher was very healthy and alert like his sister and brothers. There were 11 years between Angela and Chris and 1 year between Angela and Robert. Angela looked after her little brother very dearly and Robert was right alongside her. They grew well together. Of course, there were little tiffs at times, but nothing more than normal. They were always good students in school and always kept up their grades. Rose always helped with their schooling. Wherever they could, they used to love to help me with all the yard work: rake leaves, plant flowers, and veggies. As they grew older, they would fight to cut the lawn until I gave them each every other week. Chris was too little for that task, but happy with all the other stuff. Rose was very pleased to see us all out together. She would come out once in a while to check up on things. All good.

We still needed my extra income. As the family grew in size and age, so too the expenses. The actual physical labor of my work did not affect me as much as being away from my family. Again, I say that my attitude at home was not the best. Rose knew how I felt and whenever I showed it in the form of a bad mood, she was sympathetic to me but we both knew the need. And again, it was time to build a bridge and get over it. At times we added humor to the situation and actually, that was the best way to go.

I will move ahead a little. As our kids continued to grow and were becoming a little more independent, things were starting to improve. Both Ang and Robert became very involved in volunteer fire and rescue. They both became very active members and enjoyed years of activity and training. Angela went on to become one of New York's Finest. As I am writing about this, she just completed 19 years as of March 2019. In her first few years, Angela was learning and observing different phases of police work. Then a certain lieutenant asked Ang if she would be interested in heading up the Domestic Violence Unit and she accepted. Once she learned the so-called ropes, she loved the assignment and did very well in it for almost 10 years. Then a new administration came in, removed Angela and placed one of their own in the position. Ang felt terrible, but nothing could be done for her. Some time had passed, and Angela was approached by her lieutenant again. If she would be interested in the head of the youth program. She was a little apprehensive due to what happened with the other program. Angela took the position and again does very well with it. Because she loves to work with people of all ages and gender, there is nothing she loves more than being on patrol in a squad with a partner answering calls each day. She passed the Sergeant's exam, and due to her possibly extending her career, when 20 years are up, she may stay as Youth Officer, or she may consider her health and take a less physically challenging position. Whatever your decision Baby Girl, Mom, Pop, and Family will honor it wholeheartedly, and God will bless you.

Skipping back a little, I must add to a previous couple of pages. Both Angela and Robert did very well in grade school and graduated beautifully from high school. Angela went on to receive her Associates Degree in Criminal Justice from SUNY at Farmingdale in May 1985, did real estate and banking, but always had her heart set on the N.Y.P.D., from when she was a little girl.

Robert tried a few jobs: market clerk, electrician (which I had hoped he would take the apprenticeship) but he explained that he always had his heart set on FDNY. He took the Civil Service test which was required in New York state. After the test, FDNY did not hire at that time, but NYPD would hire. He took the position with visions of going to FDNY when they called. He completed the Police Academy and on the eve of Graduation and ceremonies, we were home having dinner when the police lieutenant called to assign Robert to the Transit Unit. He was so disappointed with that. So I said, You know Rob that sometimes when they are assigning so many graduates, they re-check and find an error. At that moment, the phone rang again with the same lieutenant re-assigned Robert to a precinct in Manhattan. He was happy for that "God-incident" but still wanted FDNY. Less than a year later, FDNY called to hire him. He was able to carry the time spent with the NYPD toward his seniority due to Civil Service ruling. More later on about Angela and Robert with some frightening situations.

Now Christopher, he also did very well in school. Prior to his graduation, he had different part-time jobs. Then, he started working steadily—first in a pizza parlor, then Home Depot which paid much more than the pizza parlor. Then Chris started thinking of his earlier years in grade school where he was bullied a lot, had no class friends, was rejected, etc. That gave him thoughts of the priesthood. Maybe there he could find some answers. Chris pursued it on his own. Mom and I were very proud and supportive of his thoughts. He went to some weekend retreats at the Seminary in Cold Spring Harbor. Chris made some new friends in the same position. While talking with some very spiritual and intellectual priests, they saw that Chris was looking for answers as to why people should behave like what he witnessed, and they recommended he should pursue the field of behavioral science. Well, he did.

He took many more courses, worked in several different facilities. Also, for a private psychologist who told Chris that he had a great gift, and to pursue the field and to get as much schooling as he can. Over the years, Chris worked hard at school and earned his Master's Degree. Chris also went on to become a Board Certified and Licensed Behavior Analyst.

Rose and I feel that the concern for others—of being victims of bullying and rejection—is what led Chris to his decision, and we did call on the Holy Spirit to help him and for us to be able to do our part as very proud parents.

Now, back to Angela. Angela married on May 21, 1988. After four years, Mr. Paul decided he didn't want to be married any longer. Not to go into detail over the breakup, but Angela's mother-in-law and all of Mr. Paul's family were very saddened over Paul's behavior, not to mention Angela's side of the family. She was very sad, very depressed. We wanted her back home and she came. She had a few different jobs in real estate and banking but felt a calling to the NYPD. So she took the written exam and was accepted pending all testing, physical fitness and performance, and was sworn in on March 1, 2000. Again, Rose and I prayed for her decision, her guidance and to trust Jesus every moment of her new endeavor. Now I know how my mom felt when my brother Vito went to war and again when I enlisted. The women of that era were the most powerful in their prayer life. I don't mean to shortchange many of today's women, for they are great too.

When Angela got settled in as to location and shifts in her work schedule, she started taking additional courses in criminal justice at LIU at CW Post and in May 2010 received her Bachelor's Degree in Criminal Justice.

Back to Robert. He passed all of his testings to enter the Department and was assigned to a house in Hell's Kitchen in Manhattan. He never talked about some of the very dangerous situations he was in, but Robert never wanted to alarm Rose and me. But we knew his job was no bed of roses. So again, we had even more to pray about and mostly to keep our trust in Jesus.

Robert married in 1992. When Robert was going to bring his girlfriend home for the first time, he was nervous. He always did his part in helping Mom clean up, never had to be told to make his own bed, etc. A really good son, and so much for us to be proud of. So when he brought her home, everything was pristine, and all went well.

Now Christopher announced that he met the girl that he wanted to marry. In 2004, Chris was another clean conscious person, just like his mother and siblings (a fine quality). We met Lisa—a sweetheart from day one. We feel very close to her—as close as a daughter. She calls us Mamma Rose and Papa Gus, we call her LiLi. It is a very refreshing relationship. They started off with an apartment in Hicksville, Long Island for about two years and currently live in a very cute, beautifully kept, comfortable and welcome-to-all home, with the love of God, in Levittown.

Now that I have introduced my children and have given a good picture of their commitments in the field of work which they preferred, and Mamma Rose and Papa Gus would have liked something less demanding, dangerous, etc. but to be out there doing their God-given gift is wonderful in our hearts, and we place them in the palm of God's hands every day. We also pray for all the brave men and women in occupations that put them in harm's way, and for anyone who has no one to pray for them. (We got you covered.) and God bless all of you.

CHAPTER ELEVEN

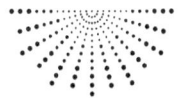

We can talk more about our 57 years of marriage. The things, big and small, which can bear heavily on each other, as our children came into having their own lives, Rose and I had more time together which was great at times, but the little nitches which would offend one or the other seemed to last longer and became more painful. One of the worst things to do was to go through the day speechless to each other. And at the same time remembering at one time we promised each other not to do that again, but I broke that promise quite frequently, and Rose would make many attempts to try to make me end it. I will truly admit that there were times I felt like a big over-grown, spoiled baby after considering the many valid attempts that Rose made to end this stupid behavior. After an episode, I felt like I threw away such precious time for both of us.

We had discussed me wanting a cabin boat many times over a long period of time—maybe 7 or 8 years. I would say to Rose, I can do all the repairs myself. I wanted a wooden boat because I couldn't afford fiberglass, and Rose's answer was we cannot afford it now. I continued to look at used boats no matter if the price was unaffordable. I was in and out of the desire, but I kept looking. One particular boat really caught my eye and I really wanted Rose to see it. Well, she did see it. Her first impression was "My God! What a monster." She saw that it had two large engines, and not knowing anything about boats, she said: "Do you think you can afford to feed the gasoline required for those two beasts?" I have to admit she was right, but I argued the point with her because I felt that no matter what boat, she would always have a negative reaction.

Then I felt that I was getting angry and my feelings were making me very uncomfortable inside, for quite a while, until I went to confession and opened up to the priest. He asked me to explain what I felt like and said, "How do you think your wife feels?" We did talk some more. I felt much better and I couldn't wait to apologize to Rose and would try to forget about boats for now.

Years went by. We had some issues, but I began to handle myself better because some of the other stupid crap could become serious again. And, there were times that it wasn't always me. I couldn't possibly mention all of the issues, but if anyone out there reading this book is married for any length of time, I would venture to say they have some of their own issues, and I hope whoever it is will find a way to get rid of the spoiled brat attitude which can be very damaging to the greatest achievement of your life as a husband, father and provider, and above all to give and receive all the love you can share.

Now one Sunday at our usual 10 am Mass, there was an announcement by the coordinator for the in-home Pre-Cana Program needing married couples to be facilitators for this program. Somehow, I knew that Rose would love to do it, but it required husband and wife to be considered. The first meeting with the coordinator was set for the Thursday of the following week and Rose had to ask me before then. I knew she was afraid that I would not participate with her. I did not wait for her to ask me. I said to her I could not possibly say no, knowing how much you had to offer on behalf of this blessed Sacrament and how thrilling that it was for both of us.

We had to go to three classes with the coordinator and his wife. We were three couples getting our format and some literature, and a date for our first six couples (5 sessions) in our home. They were given our address and starting time. We were very excited and nervous, but then it all came together.

We all introduced ourselves to each other. Rose started the session with a prayer that was required. The first session went very quickly. Rose and I discussed what we thought about how the couples felt, and wondered if we presented all the information properly. We did see a lot of enthusiasm in the couples and some said they were looking forward to the next session with us. That gave us a vote of confidence.

When each couple was asked to share one of their biggest concerns, I would get a little nervous, but Rose always was able to relate to the issue using some past experience which was quite effective. But above all, very truthful. Her method made it more relaxing for others to participate. I was really just a helper for Rose. I would try to add a little humor at times, but in the format, there were some parts where the husband would have to take on that particular area.

We both were enjoying the new venture. Over the years, we did encounter many of the couples who were happily married and most all would reflect on the wonderful experience and blessing of Pre-Cana. Rose and I averaged four sessions per year, and after 10 years we resigned to enable newcomers to facilitate the program.

God has a wonderful way of working; don't ever question Him but do realize that if you trust in Him, you will always get an answer. For me, it was the Pre-Cana ministry. It was a good eye-opener letting me practice what I was preaching. I did feel a change coming over me. I held onto a lot of things that were discussed openly and speaking with experience.

Thus concluded our Pre-Cana ministry. However, Rose did mention about checking into it at a later date—will we have the time and energy?

Rose became a Eucharistic Minister and again loved bringing the blessed host (Body of Christ) to shut-ins as well as at church and to the Queen of the Rosary Mother House in Amityville, Long Island for retired nuns. Rose had the time for this. Our children were all grown and out. I had my own involvements which were painting and woodcraft.

Then some time had passed by us, maybe six years, and a friend of mine at our work asked if I was still looking for a boat. I remained quite speechless for a moment, and Steve said, "Let me tell you what I know about it." It was a 33' 1939 Elco wooden boat that needed to be "resurrected" from bow to stern, from keel to bridge and from port to starboard, etc. I said to Steve I would like to see it. When I got home from work, after dinner, I didn't hesitate to talk to Rose. We agreed I should go look at it and to be honest with myself whether I would be able to handle it. Steve and I made arrangements for me to meet him at the boat the next Saturday.

Well, from a distance, I felt Holy Mackerel Ministry. I explained to Rose, "First, let me see the price of hauling from Oakdale to Lindenhurst." I spoke to the owner and he said, "You can have it for free." I needed title and registration after which I would have a legal bill of sale made up for the records.

A few weeks later, I cleared an area on the north side of our house where there was a tall privet hedge that helped hide it from my neighbor. When Smith Boat Hauling delivered the boat, Rose and Mom were looking out of the window and said, "I don't believe it." But then Rose said to Mom "Trust me, you will see wonders."

Now I would like to go back earlier in my writing when I was really at odds with Rose over my wanting a boat so badly, and couldn't understand why not, and actually feeling at times like a spoiled brat who could not have his way. But, as time went on, we spoke about the boat occasionally, and again, Rose felt my wanting and very comfortingly would say, "Gus, someday God will give you your desire. It may not be primo, but whatever it will be you and Him and Jesus and I know you did sacrifice." and left it up to Him. The way it came about years later with Steve was all about Jesus' Master Plan. And I thank Him every day.

The first order of business was a name for her. Several were offered and we chose Benedetto meaning blessed in Italian. I promised Rose my very best. I would give her a beautiful galley, gas stove with oven, countertop with sink, running water, electric toilet, windows all around the area, cabinet space, and sleeping area.

When I took a long, hard look at what was ahead of me, I almost couldn't believe what I took on with lots of trust in Jesus and a lot of prayers. And I know Rose was rooting for me. There is much too much to go into detail but 18 months later she was beautiful. Totally resurrected. We enjoyed her for 10 beautiful years, and whoever sailed with us shared the joy which we had. With our almost 12 years, it made her around 70 years old. Time to retire, Amen.

CHAPTER TWELVE

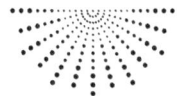

I had the desire to join our adult choir for a long time. When I would discuss it with Rose because she knew that I was very nervous about it, she would realize my nervousness and we would talk for a while. Then one Thursday night of their rehearsals, I was very hesitant to go. Then Rose said, "You prayed about it. I prayed for you. Did you ever think that Jesus may want you there?" With that thought, I went ahead and was briefly auditioned and put into the tenor section with a gentleman named Peter.

I worked up enough nerve after about one year to ask to be a cantor. The director gave me a tryout and, by the grace of God, I was accepted. I was a leader of song for about two years until our church hired a more professional director who, in turn, did not want any cantors unless they were professional—which ended my career as a cantor.

I left OLPH and went to St. Joseph's in Babylon and was accepted in the choir and as a cantor for 5 or 6 years. Then I gave it all up.

Now back to Rose, and again my chronological order is out.

Again on Sunday morning at Mass, there was an announcement that a newly opened Life Center of LI was asking for volunteers and more details were in the weekly bulletin. Come that Monday morning, Rose made her call for the information that she needed. We talked it over. They needed one day a week from 9 am to 4 pm. Here we are 15 years later, and due to some physical problems, she sadly had to give it up.

We always felt that any situation concerning each other that really understanding each other's feelings and honoring each other's wishes, and keeping things in a civil attitude is the key to real existence in a marriage. The macho man attitude went out with the last of the Mohicans. And also, that little independent attitude which we sometimes get—is at that point, don't let the encounter go sour. If it doesn't go very well, whoever is the sourface, remember you are together always and you don't need any extra grief. (Love)

Then on another Sunday morning at Mass, an announcement was made for an All-Men's In-Home Retreat given by Sister Providence Giammalvo, OP. So Rose shot me a side-eye look. I immediately got the message. It's easy to know when she is always thinking about my spirituality. Well, I enrolled for eight evenings, and we were limited to 12 men. It was given at a neighbor's house who I never knew, but by the end of the sessions, we all became close friends. It was a great experience. Sister Providence was the very best facilitator. She kept us busy with Bible-based projects, lots of Bible interpretation, etc.

At about the fifth week, she gave us all a piece of clay and we each were to form something that you remembered which you really and truly prayed to Jesus for His help with it. I immediately thought of the Benedetto from day one with her. I started praying because there was no one who I could ask things. Plenty of boats were fiberglass. I could get bits of information from boatyards or where I bought supplies, but I resorted to the library in the boat section. Well, as I stated earlier, I feel that the boat came as a ministry and the only way affordable, so I focused on one particular problem which no one could help me with. (Very important) When Sister Providence gave us the assignment, I was already toiling with a problem that I was at a point in the work where I was ready to build the cabin, but no one could help me because they didn't know. For some time when I would come home from work and be at that phase, we were in February (really cold out). After dinner, I would go out and go into the work area where my problem was. For a couple of weeks, while doing other work, I would always spend some time praying for a sign or just one little tell. When I was really at a point where I thought this is the end, and Jesus was trying to tell me something like, It's really not for you. I shut the light in the work area and began to really think about it. Then I said to myself, No, Jesus you got me to it, now get me through it, please.

I sat in the dark for awhile. Rose called from our bedroom window, "Are you alright Gus?" "Yes," I answered, "I will be in in a few." When I turned the light back on, I looked around and thought would Jesus come amidst all this debris? I gave a final look around and saw something on the port side of the hull just sticking out. Under some of the junk was a mark left on the side where the original cabin was attached. Before I went bonkers, I looked real close, took a few measurements and was sure that was my answer from the Master Builder, most everything after that was sugar and cream; and that was my sharing with Sister Providence and the retreat group. All the other men had equally joyful stories as well.

Again, if it weren't for Rose's caring, praying and understanding my determination, and giving me free rein to go forward with no complaints, it was really wonderful not to feel selfish.

Rose and I always shared our griefs and our joys. Our resentments. We had our own problems, moments of serious arguments; life together was not always Camelot. It was a reality, but you have to hang on to each other always. If you can respect your wife like a queen, she will respect you like a king (Quote: Gus). This is not guaranteed 24/7, but you will have the greatest, happiest home that you will ever know. Now, for another unhappy event in our marriage—family.

One of the worst things which we had to endure, and is still with us, is not seeing or knowing anything about our three beautiful grandchildren. They lived with us for 10 years from infancy. Now they are young adults. We don't know anything at all about them. We're out of touch with Robert's family.

Robert went on to study for Lieutenant in the FDNY, took the required tests, and did not get his results right away. 9/11 occurred, and in his company, they lost 7 men. Sometime later, Robert was promoted to lieutenant and was assigned to a house in Queens, New York. On one of his calls to a building fire, the lieutenant was first in to assess the situation. When he put on his gear, he started into the building, got halfway in and passed out. His team called medics, and thus started a long series of tests for approximately one year. They diagnosed him with a pulmonary problem equivalent to asthma. The results were to retire him on Medical. I do get the opportunity to speak with him occasionally. He assures Mamma and Papa that he keeps all his clinical visits and follows doctor's orders to the letter.

Now, about Angela.

When 9/11 came, she was a rookie with only 18 months on the job. On 9/10/01, Angela was handed a notification that changed her normal report time from 0700 hours to 0930 hours since they needed coverage for the Mayor's Primary election—scheduled for Tuesday, 9/11/01.

Angela would have already been at work, but due to that tour change, she was at home with the first plane struck the World Trade Center. Angela received a frantic phone call from our cousin LuAnn knowing Angela was at work and wondering if she was en route to the World Trade Center. When Luann heard Angela's voice and found out she was at home, LuAnn told Angela to turn the TV on. A soon as Angela found out the severity of the situation, she packed a back and headed into Manhattan—a 3-hour drive.

Angela, knowing her brother Robert was at work [FDNY—34 Engine], frantically tried to reach her brother via cell phone. However, all the cell towers were destroyed during the attack and eventual collapse of both towers.

It wasn't until later that day that Angela received a phone call from a family friend confirming he saw Robert and that he was alive (physically anyway).

Needless to say, Angela and her fellow officers spent approximately 6 months assigned to Ground Zero working 12-hour shifts. She was left with Reactive Airway Disease, chronic bronchitis and sinusitis—and prays that as time goes on, those are the extent of her illnesses—not to mention the psychological effects (PTSD) that she lives with every day.

Now, Chris.

Chris has dedicated over 25 years of his professional career to working with children and adults with autism and other developmental disabilities. He works with the individuals, their teachers and families, etc. to help them learn to be the most independent they can be. In addition, Chris is an adjunct professor and enjoys teaching and supervising students just beginning their journey.

Then there's LiLi who is also exposed to caring for special needs children and adults. She also loves her work and is also big-time on our prayer list.

Well, as parents, we were not too thrilled about the profession our kids chose, and I am not too sure if our parents felt the same about us, but they had a strong quality which was hidden by a powerful prayer conviction to have the faith they had and the trust in Jesus to let His will be done. It's wonderful giving our approval to our children. When they present you with a not lackadaisical choice, you have to figure they gave it a lot of thought. We never tried to talk any of them out of those big decisions, and we were ready to give it to God with the thought that if it's Your will Lord, (not always easy.) Arguments, bad thoughts, thoughts of failure and more aggressive thoughts can be avoided if each party listens closer to one another.

Rose and I accepted these choices of professions because we had confidence in our children and great trust in God. We often say that nothing for us or our kids was given to us or came easy for us. You get to a point where if you didn't struggle, you would feel suspicious; but it's nice to see a little beam of light at the end of the tunnel which we occasionally did see, and I truly believe that there are a hell of a lot of people out there a lot worse off than my family.

No one can make you pray or sacrifice for answers or situations which occur and why. God will always give an answer. We may not like the answer, but if we trust Him, you may see the way in which God did answer you and when He answered. In 57 years of marriage, we have witnessed so many issues in family and friends. So much of everything—happiness, heartbreak, success, serious tragedy, illness, birth, failure, death, etc. We cannot possibly touch on all of them, but we always say to each other, we cannot lose trust in Jesus and each other.

The family, starting on Day One, begins with the newlywed's vows that must be seriously taken. They say a lot of serious obligations which can be difficult to live up to. One of the purposes for Pre-Cana is to bring to those involved the importance of the promises we make to each other and be careful not to become complacent. Speaking for ourselves, we tried hard to live up to those vows before the children, and then when they started arriving. For the most part, things were going pretty good, but other sources were working, and at times, they would cloud your vision and managed to cause some unwanted bedlam. But when the smoke settled, we were the ones upset at each other and having to rationalize the situation and sometimes it didn't happen right away. Early in our marriage, I would let things go for a couple of days, and then I would think how badly Rose felt especially that we were not the cause of the problems. So I would make my apology for my behavior for letting it get the best of me.

So many things could trigger bad behavior: the job, the kids, certain people, finances, thoughts of failure in certain things, illnesses of spouse or children or family members, etc. But the very sad part of these problems is that they have caused separations because, at some point in the marriage, the vows you swore to were not taken seriously, and as we all know there is a very large population unfortunately of "my ex" generation out there, and it continues to grow.

The fact of the matter is that Rose & I feel these are some of the reasons:

1. What was the purpose of your marriage

2. Do you truly feel you were ready to commit

3. Was it for convenience

4. Was it a physical attraction (not the most important reason although some feel that it is.)

5. Was it for money or prestige

6. Was it a case that you had to get married

THERE ARE MANY MORE LAME REASONS WHY PEOPLE MARRY, these are just a few. These few reasons are not our observations, but common everyday facts.

Again, I will mention that a true and genuine commitment is very difficult. It requires not a 50%/50% deal, but a 100%/100% deal. 50/50 just don't cut it. It's only giving half of what you should really be giving.

Some of the things we feel will help keep a marriage together —and only because we experienced them:

THE HORRORS OF A SUCCESSFUL MARRIAGE

1. Fully realize that it's a blessed sacrament in any denomination

2. The main reason that we feel is—the love you feel for each other through courting. If our feelings did not continue to grow, we probably would have ended the courting.

3. The wanting to be with each other constantly

4. Totally sharing and being able to accept whatever the case, having no reservations ever for each other

5. Keeping our faith together

6. Making our home as fit as we are able

7. Sharing all of the duties in the home, even though the husband is usually the breadwinner, we still have to do our part especially when it comes to the children

8. Dealing with family on either side, trying to keep peace mainly with each other

I KNOW ALL OF THESE THINGS ARE NOT NEW OR SOUND LIKE instructions but only mentioned because some of the important issues are put aside and addressed after the marriage. That is dangerous. Usually, at that time, it becomes very difficult to mend or even not at all which can really turn into a horror show—such as drinking, heavy into sports, the "my night out with the boys" meaning I need that freedom (BS).

Be a good boy and make that time super special with the girl you adore.

The women in our lives who love us dearly are very complex, sensitive, sensible, faithful, caring, patient, possessive of valued things, honest and watchful, so why would I, in my infinite wisdom, do anything stupid or childish to jeopardize such a one-in-a-lifetime partner? And don't think that she doesn't feel that way about you (Hot Shot).

If we offend anyone of those qualities, it can be the same horrifying feeling of hurt for her as it should be the same for you.

CHAPTER THIRTEEN

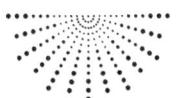

Getting back to the thoughts and concerns in our everyday life for our children, grandchildren, nieces, nephews, our friends' children. They grow up too fast when you are not in close contact with them. Before you know it, they have graduated from college, get jobs in the city for better pay, want to have their own apartment. We worry about their safety, especially the girls, but they want their independence and I would guess they feel all grown up. (OK)

In 1991, Rose had a heart attack. We were all horrified, especially the kids, until we spoke to the cardiologist who reassured us that there was no damage to the heart muscle and only minimal medication, lean diet, and scheduled checkups were needed. The kids couldn't do enough for mom; that's who they are.

There were lots of other physical problems that Rose and I kept from the three. As they grew older, it was more difficult to hide. I had my heart attack in 1999 and I was fortunate not to have heart muscle damage, but the doctor recommended and did do a stent in the RCA though. The kids, who were now older, were grateful and satisfied after speaking to the doctor.

I guess that there is little difference between frightened, horrified or afraid—either scenario can put you into a stupor. There were other physical problems we encountered over the years, but by the grace of God, until now we were spared including our children.

We continue to practice a prayerful life. Our children are happy in their marital status. Angela was deprived of the thing she wanted most in life, but found happiness at her work and continues to be trusting in Jesus. She often says Jesus has something better for me; I don't know when but I know He does. It seems that Rose and I try to offer our best help to anyone including our prayers.

We've seen and heard so much in our 57 years and the most important thing to us is from the beginning of the marriage when the mold is cast and again when the children start coming.

It is so important to be 100% truthful, patient, understanding, faithful, and above all, loving unless you want to join the (My X) Generation group.

I probably have repeated myself more than once on this matter, but it is very very important. Do Not omit Jesus, Mary, and Joseph, that blessed little holy family, please.

There is something I would like to say about all of us, married or not, just women and men. With all the great achievements in the world today, electricity, flight, automobiles, ships, space flights—6 round trips, landings on the moon, satellite communication, peacetime, nuclear energy, medicine, building Boulder Dam, tallest skyscrapers, railroad systems, Panama Canal, etc., etc., etc., the amount of science and physics, engineering which it took thousands of highly trained professionals to complete these tasks (example: a typical command module has about 1 million working parts in it.)

Now with all that super technology which man is responsible for, nothing can compare to the human body nor can it be duplicated except through procreation, a God-given privilege given to a wife "woman" and husband "man". Just two people are all it takes to produce that perfect, growing, thinking, functioning body containing multi-millions of parts, cells, nerves, perfectly formed bone structure, muscle tissue, flesh, every hair in its place, and above all, a beating heart and soul. A privilege, again, given to God's children and it must be respected by all.

The only other ingredient needed to sustain this perfect creation is for husband and wife to love, honor, respect and, above all, be faithful to each other and family for life.

(PS: I am sure that everyone who has read the previous chapter has heard all of that stuff before. It's not a lesson, just a reminder.)

There is nothing more pleasing for Rose and me as to see a young mom with her young children whether it is 1, 2, 3 or more at 9 am daily Mass, dressed nicely, well-groomed and beautifully behaved children. We know how much effort mom had to put into the occasion. God bless her, we pray. We are sure her home is peaceful. She may even be a single mom!

Then when you think of broken homes, child abuse, neglect, malnourished, horrible for the child to get behind in schoolwork all because one or both of the parents are addicted to drugs or alcohol or some other addiction and don't care about anyone else but themselves. We pray every day for those situations which are right under our noses. The greatest agony is suffered by the children. Be careful you abusive, self-centered, selfish person. Just remember God doesn't like ugly!! But he will always love you and, above all, the children, so give Him a little thank you, please!

Just think if there was a time in your life that you needed and felt the presence of Jesus. When the little ones express themselves, they cry out in fear. It is the only way they have to show us their horror. Good job folks! Chalk one up for the Prince of Darkness. Please do not let him win. He just gloats on these victories, and no one should ever give in to that so-called prince because if you do, there is absolutely no merit gained but plenty lost.

If we gave more thought to our grandparents and honored them as our heroes, role models, the best of the best, I would say that at least 90% are any one of the above. We probably have gone to them for many troublesome things and also for "What should I do Nana or Grandpa?" and be assured you would get the straight scoop. Think of those times, and hopefully, you would use that scoop. We feel very concerned for those who don't have that wonderful connection due to broken homes, family, violence, abuse. With all those odds against them, somehow they may remember at one time, there may have been some normalcy there which he or she may never forget. And probably will always have a mental picture of those two champions forever in their hearts and mind. As we mentioned much earlier, that those two couples are our first and even our only choice for our babies' sitters.

PS: there are some very willing family members available and super trustworthy, and very capable. It's all about faith and trust.

PS: And discussion made wholeheartedly between husband and wife should be felt as an honorable agreement.

PS: Don't disown anyone over a small or even big issue. If you think about it long enough, you may feel very sorry or very foolish.

PS: At times, I delude myself into thinking that I am virtuous in matters where I am actually displeasing to God!

CHAPTER FOURTEEN

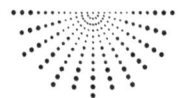

Rose and I have often said that all that we have encountered in the past 57 years and still today, we have some little glitches which are not too pleasant to deal with, and you get to a point in your life that you start hoping and praying that Jesus gives you the strength and wisdom to deal differently with matters because, at a certain age, you really don't have the octane to deal, especially when it goes out of immediate family. Dear lifetime friends are especially tender to deal with, and often times it doesn't end too happy and almost always affects you and your beloved seriously. And you two are at odds for a while. So then you start saying to each other, "How can we avoid these horrible problems which bring us grief.? "I love you." (Let's take a trip to Mars) and Rose says "Good idea, I'll buy the tickets. I'll start packing. We can catch the next shuttle. Good deal, we're out of here."

PS: Belief in God is an invitation, not a threat.

I NEVER WROTE A PREFACE TO THIS BOOK BECAUSE WHERE I chose to start, I just felt not to stop. The book is based on some tough situations and some glad times, but I tried to convey what we thought it took to make a successful 57 years together and to try to convey to you newlyweds that life is not always a bowl of cherries. And please, do all that you both can do to keep that biggest, most rewarding sacred contract you will ever make together in your lives, and with our deepest and sincere concern for you all.

May God bless you. Gus & Rose

SORRY FOLKS! ONE MORE PS:

Rose and I were thinking this morning (8/7/2019) about 7:00 am during our daily quiet time reflecting on many of yesterday's incidents and how we handled them. We came again to realize how often we thought 'How did our parents work things out?' First and foremost, from what we saw as we all grew older, the most obvious sign is that they lived for each other and with the greatest need for each other which never faltered. "All gramps are the very best." Keeping that in mind, we tried to relay the same principal to our children. If you are born into that lifestyle, all things come pretty naturally if you let them. Don't fight it. There is no better way to keep that love light burning. "Need" for each other, passionately always.

It is the best guarantee you will ever get. And don't fret, his name is written on your heart (Jesus) and He won't let you down ever, but be patient and never stop praying. And just think how wonderful it feels to be needed by someone you love. Well, again, Rose and I say good luck, God bless to all of you forever and ever.

Sincerely,

Rose & Gus

PS: I haven't said much about our son Robert and his family. Every day, Rose and I think about the situation which hereafter, more than 12 years, is still very prevalent. And with all the praying that we do and also our friends, we just keep trusting and hoping that Jesus has a better plan for all of us.

Several things enter this horrible scenario, starting from Day One when Rose and I became concerned about some things which the pair would not discuss with us or anyone else. It's not easy as parents to butt out even for the benefit of both parties. We all have premarital problems and it's always better to approach them before the nuptial regardless of the outcome. The wedding day came and went as planned and Robert set up home with us. We let them. We expanded the lower level of our high ranch as needed for the growing family as it came along. Then it became too cramped for space, so with all the happiness for the little family that we could give, they bought their new home about 20 miles east of here in Holtsville, Long Island. The little ones did not want to leave, but they soon accepted the change.

We all kept in touch. We kept up the holidays, sports events, practices, etc. All that good stuff. Then things started to go sour. We couldn't see the kids as much. They hardly came to any family function, birthdays, Christmas, etc. They were not joyous anymore until finally, we felt that the problem was serious. Well, we made many attempts to get together and resolve whatever the problem was, to no avail. It will be 12 years come March 12, 2020. We have not seen the kids since then, and that was just about the biggest horror we endure day after day. And not knowing of Robert's condition after 9-11 or knowing nothing of the kids' health or any other concerns.

Many sad thoughts go through our minds every day and some days are worse than others which can last for quite a while or until you ask Jesus to handle it for you. At times, I ask myself about the two most painful scenarios that Rose and I deal with quite frequently. Is one as bad as the other when one was brought on by deceit? And the other by natural causes. We thank God that those thoughts pass on quite rapidly, and again, by talking to each other, we can have some closure for a while and get back to a somewhat happy place.

We haven't had any joyful or spectacular events come up lately. My Chris and LiLi love to entertain at their home with LiLi's family and a few friends, and always Cousin Ann Marie and Son Christian who is not too long ago a widow and doesn't have anyone else for family. Rose and all of us agree that we will never let them be alone especially on the major holidays, plus at times, as a treat to each of us, we will go out to dinner and have a ball!!

Also, I have all of my relations in Chicago who, for a real treat, we will exchange visits. It is really refreshing to feel the love and sincerity among all of us. Time together is truly a gift. Rose has just about all her relatives in the NY area except niece Colleen in Florida who also is alone except for a few business associates, and we always wanted her here in NY. She will come up whenever possible. "She promised."

So Rose and I don't have to go very far for something pleasant to do. We try to do our best to avoid those times of sadness and at our age, I hope that there are certain people out there who realize that the clock can stop for anyone at any time, young or old.

PS: PLEASE THINK WHEN A BOY AND GIRL MEET SOMEONE FOR the first time, if there is a certain chemistry which by nature is a clue toward more interest from both parties, and in most cases is valid, but this doesn't always happen and it's not the only way people feel a certain attraction to someone. But there has to be something that creates a noticeable attraction. From that point on, the feeling must be mutual and if it is, things will come together naturally. As time goes on, through learning more of each other, good and not good, if things are worked out and not "I promise I will change" type of approach, this looks like great possibilities. But the work at this process has just begun and never really ends. Remember, the strongest bond between you two is a genuine need for each other and never take one another for granted. Always be painfully honest with each other. Rose and I always felt the need for each other. Even though Rose was always busy starting with baby John, there were times I felt selfish because they needed attention in so many things, and she was always right there. God bless these women for their great patience and understanding of their spouses. What would we do without them?

It took me many years to fully realize the importance of that once-in-a-lifetime spouse who really is in charge of the household and everyone and everything in it. The men can flex their muscles elsewhere (at the gym only.)

So my thoughts keep falling back to the most important, the unequivocal need for each other for everything.

All these events and thoughts which I mentioned throughout my writing, were somewhat a learning process for us and now we are able to share these events with someone to realize that life is not always Camelot!

PS: A COUPLE OF WEEKS AGO, ROSE AND I WERE INVITED TO A friend's barbecue with lots of people and kids. We were at a table with some people we did not know until then. Things were going really fine—lots of laughs, some family stories—the typical BBQ talk. There was one elder couple like ourselves who happened to be grandparents. Also, they have a girl 7 and a boy 3. The grandparents called the boy who was very busy playing with his toy boat. We think he didn't hear Papa call him. Papa called him again, but we could see that he was already angry and now Papa hit the table with his hand to alert the boy and demanded that he stop playing and look at him when he speaks to Papa. The little guy was frightened. He stood motionless for a moment, got teary-eyed, and put his head down while Papa continued to chastise him. Not to continue on that. No one would comment about it, but you could feel the discomfort around the table.

Rose and I spoke later about it. Not knowing Papa or the child, we came up with several thoughts.

1. Papa may not have felt well.

2. The boy may have been misbehaved at other times.

3. May have had a scrimmage with grandma at some time earlier and carried it over.

None of this behavior is acceptable, especially from Gramps. We, as grandpas, should never hurt the little ones, especially in public and away from their parents. There is no one for them to run to. Because of one of the selfish reasons we pray that Papa would realize the damage which could be done if he is not more careful with the babies.

Now, I hate to admit that I have come close to losing patience with the little ones, but fortunately, Rose was always present to stop me which I am grateful for. I know I would feel badly afterward. I don't mean to bad mouth Mr. Gramps, but only trying to show that one of these incidents can cause World War 3 with the wife, and so much better if we are always mindful of it. Amen!

PS: "Let your desires and love be guided by my wisdom, and they will never lead you to folly." (Quite from My Daily Bread, p. 193, by Anthony J. Paone, S.J.)

PS: Thinking way back when I began to write things about our marriage, our beginning, a new life together, thinking we knew each other well enough for this great commitment, well I guess we did. Here we are, 57 years later, and still seeing and learning things, sometimes wondering about each other, how we are still together after some of the real trying times which we endured. The truth of the matter is if we weren't meant for each other from the beginning, we probably would have parted a long time ago. Some couples, after being part of a lot of horrible events, may feel what the "H" did I get into, and are quite fast to split, beat feet, chow for now, hasta la vista, don't call me I'll call you, speak to my attorney. There were times that were gut-wrenching and emotional for both of us. Times when we could only turn to God to help us, and we were so glad that we could rely on His help.

Wives are always first to console. They have that special attribute which is invaluable and I certainly appreciate and admire it. Again, I repeat that the Moms are the go-to girls, and the men have their usefulness too. Haha. I don't want to keep sounding negative, so I thank God for the positive thoughts although tough at times, but good most of the time. And after the storm, please enjoy the sunshine. Remember, after any nasty confrontation, be anxious to get rid of it. Kiss and make up. Remember babe, we need each other. And from day one, we worked very hard to keep our love alive, and we will always be together.

PS: We're getting to say things like 'You are always under my feet, stand still.' 'I was calling you for a half-hour! I am right here!!' 'O my God, now what??!!' 'Where did you put the handicap card??' 'Don't forget to buy bread! OK, you told me 10 times!' 'I think you need a haircut. Make sure he trims your eyebrows.'

'I love you. I love you more!! Get a life!!!' I would like to say no more.

PS: But the items which pop up, I feel I want to share. I probably have repeated myself a few times, sorry!! I would like to mention that this whole narrative is not just about my family or Rose and me, our life together, but we are very sure that there are many people out there with some horror stories and lots of joyful stories and many not so unique.

I did mention both parents and grandparents on both sides of the fence. Mostly the impact we have on the little ones, and it goes much further. If a bad moment did occur, aside from the bad feeling on the part of the individual, but in the presence of family groups, speaking for myself I would be totally embarrassed and lost for words. Some people cannot forget those incidents.

All of the scenarios between husband and wife can be worked out when that deep feeling of "(need for each other) is there, especially when it involves the children, and they will learn from your example. Home is the best forum for learning everything you need for a good life. Thanks, Mom & Dad. Ours used to call us Bappy & Nana.

PS: Loved it and miss it.

. . .

PS: JUST ONE MORE THING WHICH TROUBLES ROSE AND ME. We pray fervently for all the young girls and boys who, by some evil-minded parasite who was able to influence these innocent souls either by cunning or by force, to become hooked on drugs. By one not caring about anything but money and being able to manipulate these victims for their own convenience. It's wonderful to know that not all are hooked but heart-breaking for the tapped ones. Also, the girls who marry or living together become pregnant and not even considering the fact that the fetus is affected by the drugs before he or she is born. If only the girls would realize what has happened to that perfect creation (herself) and what the newborn may suffer in life. Only by her self and by the help of God could this serious tragedy be changed, and in addition to that, seek clinical help. With all of the above, we pray reverently for her to return to that perfect creation which only God gives us and to find true happiness.

PS: SOME OF OUR OWN TRAGEDIES WHICH WE WROTE ABOUT are somewhat forgotten, but many remain in thought: the death of loved ones, illnesses, financial problems, family, close friends, relatives, losing a business which you loved. The most, being away from immediate family so much due to the need to be able to support home and family, etc. Some times, Rose and I would sit quietly after the kids were bedded down, and after a while, we would talk a little and usually wind up saying 'better days are coming.' And they did come.

Everything else we wrote about, for the kids of today, the importance of close family, spirituality in the home, discipline, respect, honor, family, worship at your own church, make sure you respect and honor mom at dinner. This is the time of day that Mom's look forward to during her busy, everyday tasks—laundry, cleaning, shopping, ironing, if there are any little ones to take care of, and many other duties. And then finally getting started to prepare dinner with all her love and effort for which it is always a very special occasion for her, for all to be together at dinner at the end of the day. Please, kids of all ages, do not burst her bubble. Mom deserves your attention and sharing, this is her time to express her feelings and love for you all. The #1 violator for this is texting. It is impolite, disrespectful and has a tendency to hurt Mom's feelings. Though she may not show it, it is so. Please give mom your love and just remember, Mom will always do her best never to let you down. YOU must do the same for her. God bless.

PS: ROSE AND I WISH WE HAD ANOTHER 57 YEARS. BUT THIS time to look back on every event which we encountered and think if we would have handled them differently, some the same and some with the change, but never without asking for help from the Holy Spirit Jesus.

It ain't easy but we can finally say that we are pretty much out of the doldrums. Our children are settled and happy with their work. Angela with her police. There are a few other things which would be much welcomed, but we feel it will happen in God's time and we pray that we can always accept His will. Rose always says "If you are going to pray, don't worry. If you are going to worry, don't pray." Now, that's quite simple, but not easy to do.

PS: IF WE KEEP ALL OF THE DISAPPOINTMENTS ALIVE AND NOT the joyful things, life can really be a HORROR show.

PS: I THINK THAT I DRIFTED FAR OFF COURSE IN WRITING, NOT enough of the horrors which can happen to anyone. But most of the things which concern marriage and how things should be. But these thoughts came from Rose and me which helped us avoid or handle any more horrors in our married lives. Doctors, clergy, organization, etc. all helped us see things somewhat acceptable. We both agreed that talking and sharing with close friends eases the pain even though the conversation could go in a different direction which at times was welcomed. It kind of broke the gloom. I am hoping, again, for anyone who is reading our message will find one little bit of info useful. Amen.

. . .

Final PS:

Of all the things we wrote about up until now, a few things continue to sadden us which we consider is the open wound that keeps us tight with our faith, losing a first-born baby to a dreadful illness.

Losing relations with 3 beautiful grandchildren after having them for 11 years and now not knowing at all of their well-being.

Losing a son to family issues who was the finest son any parent could ever have.

There are other things, but these are the most painful. There is not a day that goes by that one of these horrors doesn't surface to torment. The only solution is to pray, pray, pray and then pray some more. Amen.

Since our destiny was chosen by God, our faith and trust in Him help us navigate through it. It's not always easy!

Remember the three most important steps in marriage are the 3 "Cs"

- Communication
- Cooperation
- Consideration

God Bless you all forever.

Gus & Rose

THE HORRORS OF A SUCCESSFUL MARRIAGE

www.ingramcontent.com/pod-product-compliance
Lightning Source LLC
Chambersburg PA
CBHW071905070526
44583CB00016B/1849